I Love you Daddy

thoughts from a father

Eric Granitur

Sydney's Sproutin' Company
Miami Beach

Copyright © 1996 Sydney's Sproutin' Company

All rights reserved. No part of this book may be reproduced in any form whatsoever without the written permission of the publisher.

Manufactured in the United States of America
Library of Congress Catalog Card Number: 96-92403
ISBN: 0-9652844-0-9

Cover design: Randi Kwartin
Book design, setup and typography: Randi Kwartin

Sydney's Sproutin' Company
325 Meridian Avenue, #6
Miami Beach, Florida 33139
(305) 673-4332

This book is dedicated with all of my love
to Amy, my soulmate in life's fantastic journey.
This book is also dedicated to Sydney,
my sweetest of the sweet peas.

I want to thank Sydney's Aunt Lisa for
her heartfelt editing. I also want to thank
Sydney's "Aunt" Randi for bringing this book
from the roughest of drafts to what you are
holding in your hands. Randi, I could not
have done it without you.

Introduction

The genesis for this book occurred a few months after my wife Amy gave birth to our daughter Sydney. Numerous friends were amazed at how well Amy and I were doing with Sydney. Some of the new dads and soon to be dads jokingly (I think) suggested that I write a book about what Amy and I had done and were doing to help make being a parent the most incredibly exciting and wonderful adventure that I could ever imagine.

My goal in writing this book was to keep it enlightening, enjoyable and easy to read. This book is simply a compilation of some of the things I believe can help make being a father the completely joyous experience that it should be.

1

Begin to immerse yourself in the warm glow, that will shine brighter everyday, of becoming a dad. You are about to add another fantastic dimension to your life. It is a tremendous amount of work and a gigantic time commitment, but it is the greatest investment of time and effort that you will ever make. Every time you think about your soon to be born son or daughter, your smile will grow. Every time you see your newborn baby, you will know that this is why life is worth living.

❧ 2 ❧

Tell your wife that you love her at least once in the morning, once in the afternoon and once at night. You and your wife are soulmates, about to embark on a marvelous journey that will have its peaks and valleys. Let your wife know that you will always be there for her, and that you adore her.

3

Be understanding of your wife. Your wife will be experiencing mental, physical and emotional changes due to her pregnancy, most of which she cannot control, on an almost daily basis. Your wife will experience exaggerated highs and lows. During pregnancy your wife is working extremely hard carrying and nurturing your baby, who you will be holding and loving very soon. The least you can do is let her vent her emotions to you, whether they be positive or negative.

4

Tell your unborn baby that you love him or her as much as possible. You will be surprised at how strong the word love is to your son or daughter. You can never say you love him or her too much.

5

Talk to your unborn baby as much as you can. By talking to your baby in your wife's womb, you will be creating a bond with your baby. You will be amazed at your baby's reactions to your voice when you hold and talk to him or her. Your baby will know your sound.

❦ 6 ❦

Hug your wife as much as possible. The hugs can be passionate, reassuring or playful, it doesn't matter. You will be astonished by what a hug can do. It will bring the hugger and the huggee closer together physically, mentally and emotionally. I recommend getting "The Hug Therapy Book" by Kathleen Keating to refine your hugging techniques. Keep on huggin'.

7

Make love to your wife as much as possible. Your pregnant wife is nurturing your baby that is a result of the both of you being in love. There is always a wonderful radiance to a pregnant woman. Even after your wife gives birth, your passion will continue to grow. It just gets better and better. Enjoy.

8

Look into your wife's eyes and really talk to her. You both need each other for support and strength. You both need to talk to each other and express your hopes, fears, thoughts and emotions. You and your wife have to concentrate on being a team. You are both embarking on a fantastic journey which becomes even more exciting by both of you actively participating, communicating and working together.

❧9❧

Listen to your wife. During pregnancy she will need extra support from you. Support will sometimes be the simple act of giving her your undivided attention and listening to her express her feelings. After your son or daughter is born, there will be times that you will be the only adult that she will talk to the entire day. Give her a chance to talk to a grown-up.

10

Give your wife her space. Your wife needs your love, understanding, passion and support. She will also need time alone. You will know when to let her get into her own emotions and feelings. Do not feel slighted by your wife's need to be alone at times.

11

Buy your wife flowers and give them to her yourself at least once a week. There are a lot of beautiful flowers in the world and it seems that women know them all. Besides being a thoughtful way to show your love, flowers will bring beauty to your home. She will never forget that you brought her flowers.

12

Learn reflexology, which is the science of applying pressure to specific points on the soles and tops of a person's feet. Reflexology is a holistic healing technique which works on the whole person. It puts a person's body into a state of balance and harmony which in turn relieves stress. Positive changes will result throughout a person's body by stimulating his or her own healing potential. Reflexology is not difficult to learn. I recommend getting "The Art of Reflexology" by Inge Dougans with Suzanne Ellis. Try to give your wife one reflexology treatment a week throughout and after her pregnancy. You will be releasing your wife's internal energies, which will put her into a state of mental, physical and emotional balance. Your wife will love you forever.

13

Listen to classical music in your home as much as possible. Classical music really does soothe the soul. Playing classical music has made us, our daughter, our cats and our home more tranquil. Classical music creates a great background which is never obtrusive. Your entire home will feel warmer and lighter. I recommend listening to your local FM classical music station. I also recommend listening to your local national public radio station.

❦14❦

Make your home as calm as possible. Your home is where you should be able to relax and enjoy your family. You and your family will be able to find a mental and spiritual balance if your home is calm. Try to think positive thoughts which will in turn put out positive energy in your home.

❦15❦

Make your home as inviting as possible. Make your home a place where your family loves to be. Try to allow as much natural sunlight into your home as possible. Sunlight is very therapeutic for a person's state of mind. Keep your home as spacious and open as possible. Try to surround yourself and your family with what pleases all of you.

❧16❧

Exercise as much as you can. It is very important to have this time to yourself. I have found that a regular routine of exercise is a great way of keeping one's self attuned physically, mentally and emotionally. I will try to take a bike ride almost every morning and then do extensive stretching. I will also play an occasional game of ultimate frisbee. No matter what your athletic endeavor is, be it golf, tennis, racquetball or basketball, keep doing it. Keeping yourself physically active will also keep you mentally alert and emotionally fresh to be a great dad.

17

Start rising earlier. I try to get up early every morning. I find that I am able to exercise and start getting things done before Amy and Sydney wake up and my work day starts. The early morning is a beautiful time of day. Everything is so fresh and alive. There is so much hope and anticipation in the air. I also sometimes get to bed after Amy and Sydney. I find that I can recap the day and organize my thoughts for the next day before I go to bed. The night can be an extremely peaceful and magical time. You will need as many waking hours as possible to do everything you want to do.

18

Try to maximize your time. Time management will become so important during your wife's pregnancy and after your son or daughter is born. You will find that as your wife's pregnancy goes on, and then after your baby comes into the world, there will be more and more demands on your time. You will have to make careful time management decisions. Please think of your baby and wife first. As important as work and social activities are, your family should take priority. For example, if there is a choice between attending a sporting event and spending time with your pregnant wife, who could be experiencing very real feelings of anxiousness over impending motherhood, do the right thing and choose the latter. You will learn to say no and be selective in the way that you spend your time. You will also want to spend as much time as you can with your family.

❧19❧

Eat organically. I have found, through years of experimenting with food and the effects of various foods on the human body, that natural food is essential to maintaining physical and spiritual well being. You have to think of your body as a high performance sports car that will only function at it's ultimate capacity when it is given the best fuels. Your body will thank you by performing at peak performance physically, mentally and emotionally. I have become a vegetarian and try to eat only organically grown foods. Please visit your local health food store and ask for help. The people who work at health food stores are more than willing to help. I will guarantee you that you will feel better, have more energy and be able to function on less sleep. Imagine how much better your family will feel if all of you eat natural foods that are organically grown. I believe that it has had a positive effect on Sydney. Also, everything tastes a heck of a lot better.

❦ 20 ❦

Start sprouting some of your food. Learn how to sprout various wheat, bean and vegetable seeds to make delicious breads, soups and salads. The sprouting of seeds results in some of the world's most nutritious food. It is very easy to do, and beyond healthy eating it is very therapeutic to grow a seed into an alternative food source. I recommend getting "Sprout It! One Week from Seed to Salad" by Steve Meyerowitz. You will be amazed at the freshness and diversity of sprouted foods. You will be providing your family with home grown good health.

Sprouting and preparing foods from the sprouted seeds is an activity that your family can do and learn from together. Our family is now producing Sydney's Sproutin' Sprout Bread and selling it to some of the local natural food stores.

21

Barring any medical complications, please try to encourage your wife to have a natural childbirth. You will be giving your baby a great start in life. I strongly recommend that you and your wife take the Bradley Method natural childbirthing classes. The Bradley Method encourages a natural and totally unmedicated childbirth with you actively participating as coach. Your involvement is essential to the success of the Bradley Method. The Bradley Method promotes eating properly, avoiding drugs, training and preparing for labor, relaxing, providing as much knowledge as possible about pregnancy and birth, and breastfeeding. Please call the Bradley Method's national headquarters at 1-800-423-2397 to learn more about the incredible experience of bringing your baby into the world naturally.

22

Turn off the television. Television stifles creativity and puts the mind in a passive state. There are so many more productive and enriching things that you and your family can do. Just think how much more rewarding it is to read to, play with, or talk to your son or daughter.

23

Try to work at home if you can. I strongly encourage it. Please remember that you have to be very disciplined to work at home. You will have plenty of early mornings, late nights and weekends working, but in return you will be able to control the time you spend with your family. You will be taking a more active role in the development and nurturing of your baby. I assure you that it is well worth the effort to be there for your wife and son or daughter.

❧24❧

Take up hobbies that you can do at home. I took up carpentry. I slowly built a workshop in our garage. A hobby will allow you to step back from everything. You will find that it is a needed diversion at times. I have built, with lots of love, different pieces of furniture for Sydney, including a toy box, a hope chest, an armoire and various wooden toys, which Amy has either stained or painted. Each wood project has become a family affair.

25

Plant a plant or vegetable garden. Planting a garden is not that difficult to do. It is also not that time consuming. The act of tending the garden, no matter how small or large, is very relaxing and can allow you to meditate about whatever. A garden is very pleasing to be around. The planting and caring for the garden should become a family activity from which you will all learn together about the wonders of nature and learn to respect all forms of life. You and your family will have beautiful plants to look at or delicious vegetables to eat.

❧26❧

During labor, tell your wife that you love her. You and your wife are about to experience the only true miracle of life. Let her know that you love her and that you are there for her when she needs you.

27

Let your baby know that he or she will be coming into a world full of love. As hard as life might be, love is the one thing that you have to give no matter what happens. Love is the most important thing that you can give your baby.

28

You and your wife must work together during labor. Your wife will need all of the support and encouragement that you can possibly muster. This will be the hardest, most painful and most beautiful experience that your wife will ever have. Hang in there with her and never leave her side, except when nature calls. Just keep thinking that millions of women have had babies before and labor is only temporary. You and your wife are just about to receive the answer to the why in life.

❧29❧

If possible, you and your wife should hold your baby as soon as he or she is born. Touch is the most important sensation that your baby has upon birth. Hold your baby as much as possible. Except for a medical emergency, never let your baby leave your sight if you are in a hospital.

30

If your baby is born in a hospital, have your wife and baby leave the hospital as quickly as they are able to. A hospital is for sick people, not for your beautiful and healthy baby.

❧31❧

If possible, let your wife, if she wants to, be a full time mom. Your baby requires your wife's undivided attention. The contact and stimulus that your baby receives in his or her first few years will mold his or her personality, likes and dislikes, ability to learn and capacity to love. Who better than your wife to influence your baby's development?

32

Help your wife, now a new mother, any way that you can. Your wife has a 24 hour a day job. Anything you can do for her, no matter how small, will be appreciated. For example, help around the home, with the grocery shopping and with the errands. Learn how to get around the kitchen. Learn how to use the dishwasher, washer and dryer. Learn how to iron and where to throw out the garbage. Learn to ask your wife if she needs any help.

33

Try to give your wife at least one hour a day to herself, so she can exercise, take a shower and get herself together mentally, physically and emotionally for the other 23 hours. This will also make your life a lot easier. That time should be your time with your baby. You can talk to, read to, or play with him or her. With your wife prepared for the day, she will be better able to handle your baby and the endless things to do. You will also be better able to concentrate on your work, exercise, social activities and hobbies.

34

Spend as much time with your baby as you can. Every time your baby looks at you and recognizes that you are his or her daddy, you will be overwhelmed with love, and by that special something that only parents know. You will find it very difficult not to be around your baby.

35

Talk to your baby as much as possible. Since you were talking to your baby in your wife's womb, your voice is a familiar sound. If you continue talking to your baby, you will reinforce that sound and will give your baby a sense of comfort and security every time he or she hears it. You don't have to talk baby talk constantly. You can talk about anything, even current events. Your baby is more interested in the sound of your voice, the inclinations of tone and the way your mouth and lips work, as opposed to what you are actually saying.

·36·

Read to your child for at least 20 minutes a day. Please try not to miss a day. Numerous studies have concluded that reading aloud to your baby is the single most important factor in having him or her attain reading success. To paraphrase Jim Trelease, the author of "The Read-Aloud Handbook," the benefits of reading aloud include building vocabulary and background knowledge, establishing the reading connection, exposing your son or daughter to a wealth of different experiences, stimulating imagination, stretching attention spans, nourishing emotional development, introducing textures and nuances of language, and encouraging the desire to learn to read. Reading out loud also forges a strong bond between parents and children. I strongly recommend getting "The Read-Aloud Handbook." There are many volunteer organizations around the United States that believe in and are spreading Jim Trelease's message of reading aloud. Become a regular with your son or daughter at your free public library. It is never too early to start reading to your baby. Please set aside the time and read for at least 20 minutes a day to your baby.

❦37❦

Give your baby a massage once a day. The baby massage, which is a form of touch therapy, is probably one of the most important forms of communication and bonding between children and parents. The baby massage will benefit your baby emotionally, physically and mentally. Your baby will have more regular and enhanced sleeping patterns and a stronger sense of security. He or she will eat and digest food better and will develop a strong spacial awareness. You will also be more confident handling your baby. Your baby will have a more balanced development as a person. I recommend getting "The Baby Massage Book" by Tina Heinl. The baby massage only takes about fifteen minutes a day. Please try not to miss a day.

38

Hold your baby as much as possible. Holding your son or daughter will forge a bond of comfort, security and familiarity. Your baby, besides recognizing your voice, will recognize your touch, your smell, your heartbeat and your very essence. It is an indescribable feeling when your baby wants you to hold him or her. Don't forget about the hugs.

39

Get a homeopathic reference book. Homeopathy is a safe and natural medical treatment which is concerned with the whole person. Each person is treated as a unique individual. Remedies are selected on the basis of symptoms, factors which make the symptoms better or worse, disposition and appearance. Instead of suppressing symptoms, which allows the possibility of them recurring, homeopathy gets to the root cause, removing symptoms in the order in which they appear, which could result in a complete cure. The homeopathic medicines are benign and safe. I recommend getting "The Family Health Guide to Homeopathy" by Dr. Barry Rose. Although many common ailments can be self-diagnosed and treated successfully at home, others will require expert medical advice.

❦ 40 ❦

Encourage your wife to try to breast feed your baby. Breast feeding, if your wife can physically do it, is very important in your baby's development. Breast milk provides the best nutrition possible for a baby. The act of breast feeding will also forge a special bond between your wife and your son or daughter.

❦ 41 ❦

Get crafty. Remember your days of arts and crafts in summer camp and school? Well, your baby will love it too. Your son or daughter will appreciate anything that you and your wife can make for him or her a lot more than if you bought it in a store. When your child gets a little bit older, he or she will especially love anything that all of you make together.

42

Realize that your wife's attention will be focused on your baby. Your wife is now dividing her attention between your baby and you. Because you can go to the bathroom yourself, clean yourself, bathe yourself, dress yourself, feed yourself, go to work yourself, earn money yourself and generally take care of yourself, your wife's attention cannot be evenly divided between your baby and you. Your baby is now the center of your family's activities. But do not think that your wife loves you any less and doesn't want to spend as much time with you. The fact is that babies are a lot of work.

43

Keep up with your relatives. Remember that your relatives love you no matter what. They also provide a sense of security and comfort. I respect my parents much more since Sydney was born. I now realize how much love it took to have spent the time and made the effort to raise and nurture me. Also, rumor has it that relatives make the world's best baby-sitters.

❦ 44 ❦

Keep up with your friends. Amy and I have been blessed with an abundance of friends. Each friend I consider a diamond which constantly needs polishing to maintain its brilliance. Even if you cannot see a lot of your friends because of distance or other circumstances, keep up the radiance with a simple telephone call, holiday card or occasional visit. Amy and I have always found, and with Sydney it is just solidified, that it is easier having friends come over and visit us. Most everything that Sydney needs is just seconds away, and we are a lot more relaxed.

45

Get your family outside as much as possible and enjoy the wonders of nature. The best entertainment in town is absolutely free, and heightens all of your senses. You will be amazed by the look of wonderment and curiosity on your baby's face. There is so much to learn in nature. Take a deep breath of fresh air. Nature provides great therapy for the mind, body and soul.

REMEMBER THAT FATHERHOOD
IS THE GREATEST EXPERIENCE
THAT YOU WILL EVER HAVE.

PLEASE ENJOY EVERYDAY OF IT
AND ENJOY LIFE.

GOOD LUCK!